STRATFORD-UPON-AVON
and Shakespeare's Country

Birthplace of England's greatest poet and playwright, the delightful old market town of Stratford-upon-Avon attracts many visitors. Although best known for its associations with Shakespeare, Stratford, with its fine old buildings, broad streets and pleasant situation beside the tranquil River Avon, is an outstanding country town in its own right. Situated in the heart of rural England, it is surrounded by historic towns such as Warwick, Worcester and Tewkesbury and is within easy reach of the beautiful Vale of Evesham, one of England's foremost fruit-growing areas, and of the northern Cotswolds with their tranquil villages built of honey-coloured stone.

River Avon and Holy Trinity Church, Stratford-upon-Avon

Mary Arden's House, Wilmcote

Shakespeare's Country lies in the very centre of England. Its pastoral countryside and ancient towns and villages scattered around the valley of the River Avon have that essential timeless charm and tranquillity of a bygone age. The focal point of the area is Stratford-upon-Avon, birthplace of England's greatest poet and playwright. Visitors are drawn here not simply for the many famous buildings, like Anne Hathaway's Cottage (*below*), but for the atmosphere bestowed by the influence of the Bard of Avon.

Shakespeare's Birthplace is a substantial timbered Tudor building, standing in attractive gardens in the centre of Stratford. Here the poet was born in 1564 and his birthroom (*below*) can be seen, furnished in the style of a prosperous Elizabethan family. Shakespeare's father, John, a local merchant, moved into Stratford in the 1550's and he became active in the government of the town. The Birthplace, as well as being a fine example of medieval architecture, is a centre of pilgrimage for devotees of the Bard and tourists alike.

Anne Hathaway's Cottage. In the little village of Shottery, a mile or so to the west of Stratford, stands Anne Hathaway's Cottage, the birthplace and childhood home of Anne Hathaway who became Shakespeare's wife. They married in 1582 and in the hall of the cottage is the oak settle (*below*) where the couple are said to have courted. The building dates from the 15th century and is a fine example of a medieval yeoman's house. The domestic rooms are well preserved, notably the kitchen with its huge open hearth fireplace.

New Place. The attractive garden is all that now remains of New Place, the house which Shakespeare owned for nineteen years until his death in 1616. He bequeathed the house to his elder daughter but it was eventually demolished in 1759. The **Great Garden** (below) was originally the orchard and kitchen garden of New Place and a mulberry tree which grows there is said to be a cutting of one planted by Shakespeare himself. The nearby Falcon Hotel (above) contains some panelling from New Place.

Nash's House. Fronting Chapel Street in Stratford is Nash's House *(above)* which dates from 1550 although the timbered front was restored in 1912. In the early 17th century the house was owned by Thomas Nash, a local lawyer who married Shakespeare's grand-daughter Elizabeth Hall in 1626. The house is now a museum with exhibits illustrating the history of the England which Shakespeare knew. Nash's House adjoins New Place with its **Knott Garden** *(below)* where herbs and flowers are laid out in intricate patterns.

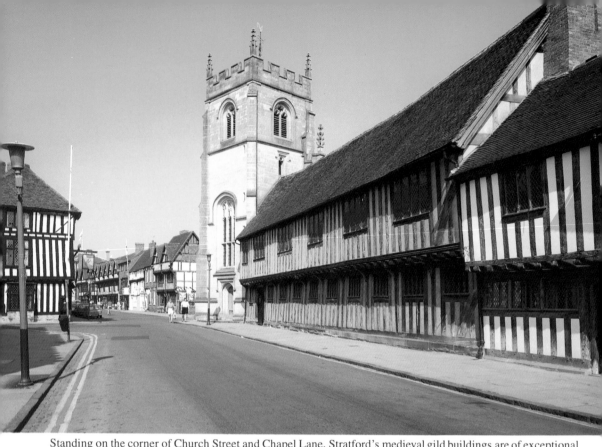

Standing on the corner of Church Street and Chapel Lane, Stratford's medieval gild buildings are of exceptional historical interest. The **Gild Chapel** (*above*) was originally built for the Gild of the Holy Cross in the 13th century but was considerably altered in the 15th century although parts of the chancel remain from the earlier period. Finest among the town's ancient inns is the magnificently timbered **Shakespeare Hotel** (*below*), a meeting place over many centuries for distinguished actors and visitors.

Hall's Croft, in the Old Town, was the home of Shakespeare's daughter Susanna and her husband Dr. John Hall. With its fine Tudor gables and elaborate chimney stacks it is one of Stratford's most outstanding Tudor houses. Behind it there is a magnificent walled garden where the herbaceous borders are filled with old English flowers. The dispensary is equipped with apothecaries' jars, surgical instruments and other medical equipment which gives a fascinating insight into 16th and early 17th century medicine.

Stratford's beauty is enhanced by the tranquil River Avon which flows lazily through the town. Spanning the river is 15th century **Clopton Bridge** (*above*) and prominently situated on the banks of the river is the **Royal Shakespeare Theatre** (*below*), opened in 1932 on the site of the Victorian building which had burned down six years previously. Downstream the graceful spire of **Holy Trinity Church** (*facing*) rises above the river. Here William Shakespeare was baptised and here, together with his wife and eldest daughter, he lies buried.

River Avon and Holy Trinity Church, Stratford-upon-Avon

Standing in the little village of Wilmcote, just north of Stratford, is **Mary Arden's House.** This excellent example of a timbered Tudor farmhouse was the home of Mary Arden, the mother of William Shakespeare. Here she lived before her marriage to John Shakespeare, the Bard's father, and the house was later left to her. After the couple's marriage, they moved into the town of Stratford where William was born. The rooms are typical of the period and include a large kitchen and hall (*below*).

Mary Arden's House, Wilmcote

The ancient town of **Warwick** is best known for the magnificent castle on the banks of the River Avon which towers above some attractive half-timbered cottages at Bridge End. The present structure dates from the 13th and 14th centuries and is one of the best-preserved medieval castles in the country. Warwick contains many other notable buildings including Oken's House *(above)*, the 16th century home of a wealthy merchant who founded almshouses in the town, and the East Gate *(below)* which is one of two remaining medieval gateways.

Bridge End, Warwick

Royal Leamington Spa is a delightful inland watering place situated adjacent to Warwick on the River Leam. Beside the Leam Bridge stands the Royal Pump Room (*above*) where the natural medicinal waters can be taken. The town is noted for its Regency buildings and beautiful gardens, principal of which are Jephson Gardens (*below*) with their fine lawns and flower borders. The main street is a broad thoroughfare known as the Avenue which is dominated by the distinctive town hall dating from 1883.

Between Leamington and Coventry is the small town of **Kenilworth**, famous for its massive castle, once a rival to Warwick but now ruined. The great Keep (*below*) dates from the 12th century and the castle was originally surrounded by an artificial lake. The fortress was one of the greatest strongholds in England and during the Baron's War only fell to the army of Henry III when the defenders succumbed to starvation. In the 16th century the castle was turned into a palace by the addition of fine domestic apartments.

Around Stratford-upon-Avon there are numerous charming villages where black-and-white timbered cottages abound. The splendid old homestead at **Wick** *(above)* is typical of the architectural styles of rural Warwickshire. Some four miles from Stratford, the village of **Welford-on-Avon** *(below)* is encircled in a loop of Shakespeare's River Avon. Here thatched cottages line the main street and cluster around the church while **Overbury** in Worcestershire is rich in elegant stone houses with attractive gardens.

Cottage at Overbury

The Almonry Garden, Evesham

Evesham is a picturesque town on the banks of the River Avon. Its historic buildings include the timbered Round House and Almonry, and the 110 feet high Bell Tower (*above*) last remains of a once great Benedictine abbey church.

Close to the pretty market town of Alcester stands magnificent **Ragley Hall** (*below*). Set in 500 acres of parkland, landscaped by Capability Brown, the 18th century house contains superbly decorated rooms, including the magnificent Great Hall.

Shakespeare's **River Avon** meanders through the heart of rural Worcestershire and Warwickshire. It is navigable for pleasure craft from Stratford to its confluence with the River Severn at Tewkesbury, and offers an excellent means of sampling the delights of the area. Some six miles below Stratford the river flows through the pretty village of **Bidford-on-Avon** (*above*). After Bidford the Avon crosses the Worcestershire borders and flows down through Evesham. Below the town the river is traversed by **Hampton Ferry** (*below*).

To the south of Evesham the river skirts 960 feet high Bredon Hill below which nestle many of the most attractive Worcestershire villages. As it passes through the ancient market town of **Pershore** it is spanned by two bridges including a fine 17th century brick structure (above). Dating from the 11th to the 14th centuries, **Pershore Abbey** (below) is now used as the parish church. The presbytery vaulting is remarkable and there are also some beautiful Norman arches.

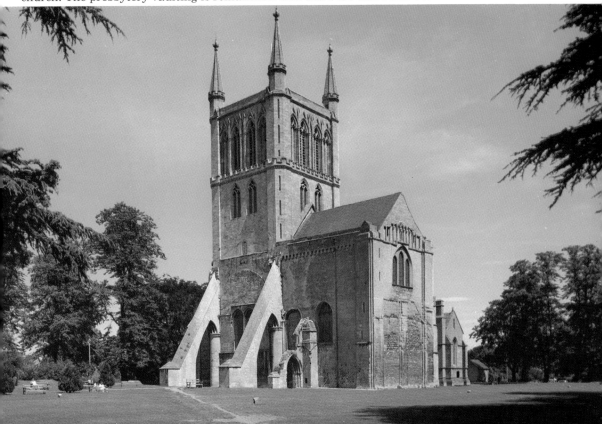

Standing above the banks of the River Severn is the fine Gothic cathedral of **Worcester.** Begun in 1084 the cathedral has an 11th century crypt and also contains the tomb of King John, buried here in 1216. The city was the scene of one of the last battles of the Civil War in 1651, where Charles II's forces were defeated by Cromwell. The timbered Commandery was the Royalist headquarters. Situated in the world famous Royal Worcester Porcelain Works is the Dyson Perrins Museum, with its fascinating collection of English china.

The picturesque town of **Tewkesbury**, with its half-timbered houses and old streets, stands at the confluence of the Rivers Avon and Severn. It has a long history and was the site of one of the great battles of the Wars of the Roses in 1471. Tewkesbury's greatest glory is the magnificent abbey church which has the largest Norman tower in England. The abbey was saved from destruction in the 16th century when local people purchased it from the crown for £453 – it has remained the parish church ever since.

On its southern fringes Shakespeare's country adjoins the northern edge of the Cotswold Hills, a land of rolling downs and unspoilt villages. **Chipping Campden** *(above)* boasts some of the most perfect medieval Cotswold architecture including the 15th century Parish Church and a particularly fine vaulted Market Hall which dates from 1627. **Broadway** (below) is deservedly one of the most famous of all Cotswold villages and the art of Cotswold building is seen at its best in this outstanding group of 15th century cottages.

Picturesque **Bourton-on-the-Hill** *(above)* lies in the north-east of the Cotswolds and has a straggling main street lined with delightful old cottages. The church contains the Winchester Bushel and Peck, a standard measure used in Tudor times for settling disputes relating to rents and tithes. The small but thriving market town of **Moreton-in-Marsh** *(below)* grew up along the line of the Roman Fosse Way. The stately Market Hall stands prominently in the middle of the highway near a small green where the village stocks still stand.

Dating back to Saxon times, **Banbury** *(above)* is a charming mixture of the old and the new. Situated some twenty miles from Stratford-upon-Avon, the town is perhaps best known for its Cross, the original of which was destroyed in the 17th century by the Puritans and replaced by the present neo-Gothic structure in 1859. The Oxford Canal was authorised in 1769 to link the Warwickshire coalfields with Banbury and Oxford. Banbury Lock *(below)* lies in the heart of the town and is used today mainly for recreation.